ALIVE TO DEATH

ALIVE TO DEATH

by

MICHAEL HOLLINGS

MAYHEW-McCRIMMON
Great Wakering

First published in Great Britain in 1976 by
MAYHEW-McCRIMMON LTD
Great Wakering Essex England

This edition 1981

ISBN 0-85597-107-X

Cover design: Neil Summerland

Printed in Hong Kong by
Permanent Typesetting & Printing Co., Ltd.

To Sheila, Kit and all the others who have helped me to write this book by their friendship and the way they live.

CONTENTS

INTRODUCTION

My reason for writing this short series of ideas is the hope that it may prove to be a source of light, strength, reassurance and joy for those who come across it.

Being human, like anyone else, I cannot escape meeting suffering in myself and others, and meeting death in others, in my own friends and relations, and sometime in myself.

Suffering and death raise in us all kinds of differing emotions. There is fear and dread; there is concealment; there is the 'couldn't-care-less' attitude; there is bitterness at being struck down, and the bitterness of relatives; utter desolation, the 'end' not only for the one who dies, but for the one left behind. And then other attitudes and reactions, not perhaps so often seen: the fear giving way to peace, when a person has been told the truth; the deepening of feeling, sensitivity and humanity as death is faced; the happiness of last months, weeks and days, enjoyed together by a husband and wife, facing the death of one partner together. And so on.

Situations arise for a whole number of people, when one person comes 'under the doctor', and the disease diagnosed is of a terminal character. Consultants and doctors have to think out whether to conceal the truth, or tell the patient. Nurses may know, and may be 'bound' by the decision of the doctors. Parents or close relations, husbands, wives, adult children may be faced with a strong desire 'not to tell' the sick person how bad he is, and especially not to mention a dread word like cancer; in this they may be supported or even swayed by the advice of the doctor. And, of course, there is the 'patient' who may know nothing, may suspect, may be afraid to ask, may be clutching at straws.

So often, everyone enters into a 'let's pretend world', with those in the know encouraging the sick person to a hope which is more likely to be fulfilled miraculously than medically.

In this way, those who have been for many years joined in complete openness and trust suddenly find themselves faced with deceiving the partner, the brother, the friend, the child they have loved so dearly.

Now, I write because in a way I have been fortunate or unfortunate in experiencing a very marginal part of personal suffering and fear of death; and in having a very long and wide experience of other people's suffering, fear, hope, joy and death.

I want first to record very briefly for you a few of my personal experiences, because I hope in some way, directly, obliquely or in contrast, they may help you to grasp your own experience, face it, and then, whatever it may be, grow in it and from it, through suffering and in joy.

My first experience of death, when I was about seven, was not in a person dying, but in a dog. It is sad to me, but I am afraid true, that the death of the dog was far more vivid and distressing than the death of my Father, both of which occurred as 'early memories'. The dog was run over. Somehow he struggled a considerable distance back home, and when I saw him first, lay panting his life away by the wall of our house. He was only a mongrel, but he was real. The gathered family and friends lamented, but did not seem able to do anything except call the vet. What did I feel? Well, memory says I felt helpless, because I wasn't allowed to touch him, and everyone was just saying 'Poor thing', and 'What a shame' . . . and I did not know why the big grown-up world didn't or couldn't do *something*. I was angry, defeated, heart-broken and filled with a kind of hatred against '*them*'. And part of me was mercifully numb, so that after a day or two, I was quite OK again.

Later, on a human level, I was in a car crash as a young teenager. My mother and sister were both concussed, I was all right, but an older man in the front seat was badly hurt. That night, I was alone at home with my mother and sister, both of whom were shocked and not too well. I was in torment that night, and in a way alone, fearing for my mother and sister, and dreading that the older man might die. I felt 'dirty' somehow, and 'responsible', and angry, especially when the man did die, despite all my prayers.

The first time death came near to touching me was in World War II when I was hit in the neck in a Tunisian field, thought I was dying, survived, walked back to an advanced dressing station, and then after an ambulance ride, lay on the floor of some farmhouse for what seemed like days, numb, fearful, listless, drifting, and terribly sore. Just before I was taken to be operated on, an orderly bent over me: 'D'you know so-and-so?', he said,

'Wounded just where you are. Just died, y'know!' . . . and I was carried in for the operation . . . and my memory says I could not have cared less if I was about to live or about to die. Nothing worried me. I was tired, tired, tired, without apprehension. I did not consciously fear death. I was just tired.

When I recovered, I was fairly constantly 'in danger'. And I had lost my belief, my Faith. I kept having people killed beside me, or missed death by a few feet. I got nervy, cowardly and afraid. I hated and dreaded going to the front line; I kept down, I had to force myself out, so that I was not for ever too frightened to move.

My own experience made me protective of the men and their lives. I suffered for them, as well as myself and tried hard to help the wounded and the dying, and also those whose nerves got frayed or broken. It was a horrible period and experience.

Then, in the middle of fear, I had a chance to escape. The casualties were so heavy in two battalions, it was decided to amalgamate. I was adjutant of one, and those who had served longest were to be sent home, others to go on fighting in Italy. I was due for home, and this coincided with a letter from my mother saying she had inoperable cancer, and could I get home. It seemed to fit. Then, my opposite number approached me. He explained that he was forty and had a wife and four children in England, whereas I was only twenty-two and single . . . could we change places? It took me a good bit of struggling, both through fear and through longing to get to my mother, but eventually I agreed to stay. I think that decision did something to me.

Eventually I saw my mother in England at the end of the war, managed to be with her as she moved towards death in pain and fading strength, and then, before she died, was shifted out to Palestine. She died while I was there, and they would not let me home, so that I had the pain of lonely distance outside Haifa, and I don't mind confessing that I cried myself to sleep in my tent on several nights.

But it had the effect of crystallising God's rediscovery of me, as I tried to re-assess myself and life after war, after her death, and faced by the problems of all the men under my command, many of whom were even more lost than I was.

A period of life came to an end. Some of me died. I had a bout of crippling sinus trouble, plenty of time to think, and the crisis of defence duties in a country developing from Palestine to Israel.

It brought me to opt for God . . . and to decide to try to be a priest.

In priestly life, I have done no more than be about and attempt to be open to whatever and whoever came my way. It is normal for a priest to spend a considerable amount of his time with the housebound, the sick in or out of hospital, the dying. It is normal to move among those who have suffered bereavement, to be often at the registrar with relatives of a deceased person, to be often at the undertaker, to be often at the funeral, the graveside or the crematorium . . . and to be with the re-adjustment to life of those who continue to live after the one they loved most of all in the world has died.

In this, it is natural that many different aspects of

human reaction emerge. Over and over again, I find myself in wonder and awe at the beauty, hope, love, joy and faith which emerge. I find myself saying; 'If only I could have her courage', 'If only I could have his patience and faith', 'If only I could accept suffering and go on being so cheerful and happy', 'If only I could die so serenely joyful as that child'.

And then there is the other side. The time when someone reacts in sheer, naked terror, resentment, bitterness and anger. There can be complete self-absorption which alienates everyone, friends, relations—husbands from wives. The time when physical anguish wracks a person till he pleads for release, or mental torment drives another beyond the brink.

And apparently all anyone can do is to sit and cry out to the God who does not seem to be there (or if he is, to care): Have mercy. Do *something!*

All this experience, as it gradually built up, seemed to make me in every way a pigmy . . . but a pigmy who wanted more and more to be about, to help, even by being helpless, to guide if the Spirit, not I, moved.

In a way, I am sorry to have inflicted all this on you as a kind of justification for writing at all. Have you ever been in that position? Where you are so hamstrung, so inhibited, you feel so stupid and so empty, you are so full of self-pity for yourself . . . and yet you *want* to express *something* . . . or *someone* wants to express to you.

It may be *pain* . . . just stay here . . . it helps . . .

It may be *loneliness* . . . I'm afraid . . . don't go away . . .

It may be *despair* . . . I'm so empty . . . I'm in a

panic . . . Help me!

It may be *peace* . . . stay quietly with me, and speak of God.

It may be *love* . . . I love you so much. I can do nothing . . . but *be here*.

I just hope and pray that what is written here will convey something to you. If it is something felt and responded to, Thank God.

If it is disbelief . . . pray.

If it is a feeling I have got it all wrong . . . write and tell me so.

For I want to put before you the full humanity of man, woman and child, as shown in the real Jesus Christ . . . God and Man . . . because:

'Although he was Son, he learnt to obey through suffering; but having been made perfect, he became for all who obey him the source of eternal salvation . . . *(Hebrews. 5.8-10)*

Michael Hollings

FACING MYSELF

Life is a very absorbing thing.

By that I mean that every man, woman or child I have ever met is very busy living, except for those who are busy dying.

Of course, many of these people, and people in general, are not aware that they are busy living or dying. As far as they are concerned, they are just going on living, making the most of things, thoroughly happy as they are, just waiting to win the pools, planning for next summer's holidays, expecting the new baby . . . and so on.

I suggest, at this point, you yourself could well stop a minute or two . . . because I suppose you are reading this book. And if you are, to stop for a minute or two will be no more waste of time than going on reading! Stop for what? Simply to ask yourself what you are doing with life . . . your life . . . ?

I take it you *have* now stopped and thought. If you haven't, either throw away this book, or go back and begin again. *If* you are interested, follow the instructions. If you are not . . .

Now, the point of this tiresome, irritating passage is literally to irritate or to intrigue you. If I have your attention, then I hope we shall get somewhere.

All too often, men and women, you and I, do not stop to think out what manner of creature we are.

As far as we go, we go. There are so many aspects of living which just have to be kept pace with; there is no time for anything else.

And so, we do not stop to think that we will die . . . there are too many problems in living, keeping going, keeping up with the Jones's.

You may have heard of the headmasters who were discussing what education was about: what do we educate young people for? They all gave answers like character building, to make a place in the world, to get a good job or profession etc. Finally one remained. 'What about you?', they asked. 'Oh I educate them for death', he replied.

Morbid? Well, it could be. But that depends what kind of a person you think you are, what life is about, whether there is anything after we die.

Generally speaking, we get pulled up sharp when someone close to us suffers or dies.

There may be life after death, there may not be life after death. As far as I know, no one can prove that there is no life after death, though it is fairly easy to slide into accepting 'there can't be, . . . what proof has anyone that there is?'

Well, taken just on thinking, looking, reading, discussing and so on, there is no *proof*. It is a matter of believing. But the person who believes in life after death has the vast amount of humanity, history and perhaps evidence on his side. The evidence can be culled from anthropology if you are learned, and from the attitude of ordinary people down the ages, if you are ordinary yourself. There are also many half-questions, hints and unfathomable puzzles in science, the exploration of space, extra-sensory perception and so on.

Above all, there is the history of religion, which can easily be held up to mockery and pooh-poohed, but which has a disconcerting way of itself rising again as a problem, much as it asserts resurrection from the dead.

Belief in life after death is difficult. It may seem more difficult for you than for many. In that case, be of good heart, and do what you can to open yourself to belief in Jesus Christ. Because he is the strongest possible proof of life after death.

I cannot here and now go into a long suggestion of how you get to know him. I just suggest that if you do know him already, you ask him to open you up until you also know yourself in knowing him more. Then I suggest you leave yourself open to him, by waiting on him, especially in your times of pain, anxiety, loneliness or despair; but also when you are joyful, and warm and filled with hope. If you do believe, see that you can also enormously help the person near you who does not have belief... not by preaching at him or her, but by being quietly serene, and being prepared to be with them. Perhaps the strongest phrase to be repeated over and over again to oneself is 'God loves me, God loves me, God loves me,' and to the other: 'God loves you, God loves you, God loves you'.

If you do not believe, what should you do? Still face yourself as you are, and think quite straightly of living and of dying. What makes for happiness and fulness? It may be hard to accept this with part of us, but deep down it is true that we get more happiness by working and striving than we do from sitting and moaning or resenting. If you live as fully as you can here, then the fulness should include others, your work and care for them, and the giving of yourself, rather than the preserving of yourself.

We are all expendable, because we are all dying. The greatest human dignity is being able to co-operate in giving ourselves away in loving others, just as Jesus Christ did . . . then dying is our glory and leads to a fulness of life beyond our dreams with the risen Jesus. So, in brief, quietly face yourself, your sickness, your pain, and anything that hits you. Do not run away. If everyone else deserts you, and you lose yourself in despair . . . He is still with you . . . He still loves you. Courage. Trust. Hope. Love.

THE CONSPIRACY OF SILENCE

I write as a person who believes in God and in life after death. I do not write as an expert, and I cannot tell anyone much about life after death. But the conviction, faith or whatever you would call it is strong in me.

However, when it comes to what I have already referred to as the conspiracy of silence, it is essential to face the fact of unbelief and belief running side by side in hospital wards, among doctors, staff and patients.

This means that any general assertion that 'the patient should never be told' or that 'the patient should always be told' falls down immediately in its credibility, because it does not take account of the individual.

By and large, death is very individual. We may die 'in a group' through accident or disaster, but even so, we die individually. Many people die completely individually, in that though there are many, many others in the world we know dying at the same moment in time, here and now, in this room or ward or street or factory, this person is the only one at the point of death.

It is a truly human emotion to be afraid of death, or perhaps more properly to be afraid of dying.

I do not think any human being should be ashamed of being afraid. I almost feel that, to begin with anyway, it is the one who can say 'I am not afraid of dying' who may be a little less human than the one who says 'I am afraid'.

But I also think, and *know* from a great many individual experiences, that the average human being, believer or unbeliever does not always fear, or after initial fear and even panic, adjusts to the confrontation with death in a remarkably resilient, though often individually different way. As an example I quote from the last letter of a woman who died of cancer in 1974:

Dear Holly,—You sent me such a good letter—I do want to answer it.—The problem of dealing with this fellow, Death, has been interesting. (Funny—what would women's lib say to my making Death masculine—but surely I can't think of myself being swept up by a lady.) In the first place, when I saw him come striding up to my house, garbed in all those strange garments we humans have wished on him, I wasn't in the least scared. I opened the door and we had a nice little chat. Subsequent talks have been reassuring and I know he's my good friend. I'm sure you must have a nodding acquaintance with him, so you have the same feelings. ('To talk of holy things.' Richard Sewall, *Reader's Digest* Feb. 1976.)

After the kind of experience that I have had in life, I am going to stick my neck out and fly a few kites about attitudes and approaches.

I know I can be attacked as not knowing what I am saying, but the whole matter is literally of such vital importance that I cannot be quiet. I say 'vital' and I mean it, because we are responsible for justice to each other as human beings, and either on godly or humanist reasoning, each person has a right to live and die with dignity, and it is for this that so many, thank God, are striving in today's world.

CONSULTANTS AND DOCTORS

A very sensitive and skilled and caring consultant was talking to me recently about inhibitions which doctors have about telling patients 'the worst'. He admitted that there were many reasons, good and probably bad as well. And he suggested that often a trained 'professional' did not like admitting that he was beaten, and whatever he might say, this very probably lay behind his reluctance to admit defeat.

I am sure there *are* many reasons, like difficult prognosis. But this one is a good model. Facing it, it is possible to see all kinds of good reasons, good, that is, for the patient, in keeping up morale, giving hope, maintaining confidence in the doctor, etc. But I think it is important also that we see the personal and human in us, which suggests to us that we are protecting the patient, when in reality we are protecting ourselves.

I am sure that humility is needed at all levels. The relation between the various 'hierarchies' of hospital life and 'lay' or patient life is not always sufficiently developed for the kind of trust which is needed. It must be extremely difficult, with the lack of time and the numbers involved, to get to know each patient sufficiently closely to be able to give them time to express their hopes, worries and fears, or even to make a space for them to unburden their cares on you.

Yet 'being with' is an almost essential ingredient, if the 'scaredness' in face of the 'big man' is to give way to the kind of admission of concern and fright which needs to be released.

Over and over again, the comment is 'Oh, but he is so busy!' 'I could not burden her with my little worries' . . . when the 'little worries' are in fact suffering, the facing of death and the surrounding fears . . . little worries indeed!

MATRONS, NURSES AND WELFARE STAFF

The 'being with' also involves those who are perhaps more often about in the wards, if a person is hospitalised—or at home, if the sick man or woman is there. Very normally, the difficulty of continuing a deceit or the possibility of developing a 'healing' relationship is more immediately present.

What can be said, the attitude that can be taken, the conspiracy or the openness . . . these things depend largely upon those who are 'above', and naturally the more there is understanding and sharing and teamwork at all levels, the easier and better the relationship which develops.

I cannot legislate. I can only point out the strain all round which can result from a failure to face the situation, or an attempt to cover up the truth.

Now, I know that there are and always will be those who do not want to face the truth, but there should be serious consideration of the 'availability' of the truth, even though the situation may never appear right for revealing it, or else the patient may seem to be saying 'Don't tell me; I don't want to know'.

It is at least worth considering and discussing

whether someone who does not want to know does not, in fact, also have the ability to discount or forget what he or she does not want to hear.

In all this, there are human beings living with, helping, caring for and loving other human beings. All of us are more or less prone to the same weaknesses, the same fears, the same hopes, and the same despairs. Each of us to some degree has the same shyness, especially in revealing ourselves and our cowardice; each of us hesitates to 'intrude' upon or 'burden' another person.

The wonderful truth which we can all learn by practice is the cost and the gain of sharing . . . with the gain always seeming in the long run to outdo the cost!

It is, if we just sit down and think about it, a very wonderful thing to belong to the species *homo sapiens*, to be human, to be a man or a woman or a child, to be able to laugh and to be able to cry. And each of us is one of these lucky people.

I will always remember trying to help a fifteen year old lad who had terminal cancer. His mother had died of cancer, his father had left home, his brother and sisters were in an orphanage, and when I first knew him he had already lost a leg through carcinoma.

People were kind to him, and gradually he came from a frozen refusal to communicate at all through to cheerfulness and acceptance even of pain. One day when two of his friends were to be married in Ireland, I suggested he sent them a greetings telegram. He was delighted, but said he did not know what to say. I left him to it. Presently he wrote out the message . . . 'To two very kind people from a very lucky boy, wishing you every happiness'. Perhaps few people would think it possible for such development, but all those who are really involved know the tremendous depths and strengths and tendernesses of the human being.

All those professionally involved with the health or sickness of each and all of us has a continuous opportunity for 'healing' the spirit, even when the body is falling apart. Oh yes! It is demanding, all right, and I remember towards the end of his life, with this same lad that he said to me one day, when we had been talking about death; 'you know, I wouldn't mind dying, if you were dying too' . . . which led on to a joyful link up with his mother who had died and so on.

Part of concern and sensitivity is to feel so much for and with the other person that decisions can be made, and silences can mean deep things, and confidence grows.

AUXILIARY HELP

It is not always appreciated just how much really human contact comes not from the professionals, but from all those other people who are about in hospitals. From my own brief experiences as a patient, and also from 'being about' in many different hospitals, I *know* for myself the extraordinary comfort of the 'tea lady', the kind person bringing round books or sweets, the cleaner, the man pushing the trolley down to the X-ray or the operating theatre.

Normally, these people are taken for granted. If any one of them happens to read this little book, then I hope they will realise that their down-to-earth concern, humour, interest and care can do and does a huge amount for those who may be living in an 'unreal world' which is not really unreal, but builds up round the professionals.

I believe these very ordinary, very solid, very real people have a part to play, which they should be encouraged to play, by being helped to feel a real part of the team or community, working for the good health of all.

This, of course, applies even more strongly in regard to those patients who are living at home. The presence and the care of those looking after meal services, the wonderful extension of their scheduled duties by home helps . . . these are all of almost incalculable value when there is a positive and loving dimension to what is being done.

Naturally, this should extend even further, and this is discussed in the next chapter.

THE COST OF LOVING

St Paul has his very well known and extremely beautiful passage on love in his letter to the Corinthians. It is often read at weddings, and as a priest I have frequently tried to comment on it in such a way as to be useful to bride and bridegroom on a day when everything is so important. It all may become trivial and insignificant.

The opening phrase of his exposition of the qualities of love is:

Love is patient.

Speaking at a wedding to a couple about to pledge themselves in front of their friends and relations to love 'till death do us part', I find myself dwelling on this phrase: Love is patient. It sounds pretty dull compared with what the poets and the pop singers declare.

But suffering and love go hand in hand, if the love is going to be co-terminus with living. That is why the pledge given and taken is 'for richer, for poorer, in sickness and in health'.

Married love is a 'model' of loving, but a model which has its effects through the whole family, upwards to grandparents, downwards to children and grandchildren . . . in a well-knit family, everyone is in it together, with in-laws as much part with the other side of the family as any blood relative.

It is normally within some kind of 'family'

setting that we live and die, though there are numerous and sad exceptions such as marriage breakdown, illegitimacy and orphaning which take their toll.

Allowing for frequent exceptions, and for the need to take each situation as 'special', the basic question is one of the way in which 'the family' take and live out the news that one of its members is sick unto death.

Now, this is a situation which is intimate as few other situations are. For this reason, I am writing these words. Does anyone have the right or duty to 'interfere' in such intimate matters as the sharing of the dying of the loved one?

I find this almost intolerably difficult to answer. I know quite well what my own experience and mind/heart says. I would always want to know myself if I was dying. I would always want those I loved to share this with me. And if it was someone other than myself who was dying, I would want to be able to share with them the knowledge of their dying.

But having said that, I do know the pains and pressures which are present . . . from doctors and nurses, from relatives and friends, from the scaredness within me. How I hate pain in others! Though I know myself, I cannot know others just like that, but only by being with them and building relationship.

It is at this point that it is helpful to think of two things. The first is whether on hearing news of my brother, my mother, my friend I immediately think *only* of him or how far reaction is coloured by myself and my own feelings. Naturally, the human that is myself is always partly at least, self-centred. But the love we have been talking about is really other centred, and includes the element of suffering, which I must undertake (gladly if possible, but undertake anyhow) for the other.

This means that the whole way I live and the attitude I manage to cultivate, especially through prayer and facing up to life, will make a difference to the way I accept news of illness, and the approach of death. I am, therefore, urgent that we each of us continue or begin to try to be less self-centred, more concerned for the real dignity and fulfilment and joy of the other.

But this ties up with the second point . . . a need we each have to think through the nature we possess, with its inevitable involvement at some stage with death. And in this thinking, we must ask ourselves directly whether death is the 'last indignity' in human nature, or whether contrary to current secrecy, hiddenness and fear, it is (or perhaps can and should be) the 'last dignity'.

Can you see how this attitude and atmosphere is best built into our whole way of life all through, and that we cannot afford to wait for the crisis before we face the issue? Older, and some would say 'more primitive' approaches to death by their very openness and ritual teach children from early days to expect, live with and not fear so much, the advent of death in the family. There is a very great importance both in early acceptance and also in some kind of ritual which can express honour, dignity and grief all together.

With our secrecy, our in-out-muted-crematorium-ritual of today and our inability to 'be with' grief and grieving people, we are causing a very considerable damage to a great many.

It is important for anyone who is reading this to sit and seriously consider his or her attitude to death and dying. Please do this. The happiness of yourself and perhaps quite a number of others depends upon your openness.

When you think of it, there are so many different things which the 'dying' person might want to complete, even in the area of people with whom there have been quarrels, unsettled business, debts to be paid off. And then time and again, I have come across the situation where this crisis faced together has given a husband and wife, for instance, a whole new growth in relationship, to a depth and fulness which they had never experienced before.

This is not to say it is all easy, but it is the path of love where it has come to be accepted that the more loving attitude is in sharing rather than in concealing. I know, because I have met many of them, that there are contrary opinions and reasons against sharing, but I can only say from the experience which I have had over the years, I would put my weight behind sharing rather than concealment.

The acceptance of openness, sharing and facing sickness and even death does mean the acceptance of patience, suffering along, suffering with, love, listening, waiting, and many other facets which can only be lived as they are met.

In this, there is no doubt in my mind, because I am a believer in the relationship of God and man, that prayer, the love and service of God, the acceptance in belief of the after life, and the general approach to life, death and resurrection in Jesus

Christ is the most important and vital of all factors.

Here it is necessary to learn to pray, to learn to listen, to learn that the 'just man lives by faith'. But it is a way open to all, even though it is the way of the cross, embracing the 'man of sorrows' who has, through God, emptied himself to share completely our sufferings. He knows what your suffering is about . . . he has felt it himself, and been through the facing of death in others, and also in himself.

The development and closeness of relationship between God and man, man with himself, and men and women with each other is central to the right outcome, because we have to become sensitive to each other. There is a time for all things. Normally, it is as well for the sick person to come through to realisation, and to be helped towards it by the open attitude we have. Sometimes we can broach the subject simply and directly, often we need to wait, to listen, to be available for questioning, not hiding or prevaricating.

And all the way, love of the other, true love which admits the place of suffering, must prevail, especially over our own fears and pain. But this is immensely helped if you can believe in the resurrection, because then you can feel the support of the wonder of eternity, brought so near in the compassion, love, suffering and rising of Jesus Christ.

HE IS GOD OF THE LIVING

As Christians, we believe that life continues after death, though we are not always very successful in any attempt to picture it to ourselves. Indeed, many of the 'pictures' of heaven are more likely to kill enthusiasm for an after life than to encourage the ordinary human being to 'long to be dissolved and to be with Christ'.

However, I do not want to dwell on the after life at this point, because these last words are about those who continue to live in this world as we know it, rather than about those who have passed through death to life.

Yet, there is a sense in which we each of us pass through death or have a little touch of death when someone close to us dies. It is for this reason that I want to stress the aspect of resurrection which is central to Christian living for that period which any one of us continues to live as orphan, as widow, as lonely at the separation of the grave.

Mourning is good, weeping is good, but not as a permanent extension of living. Though there can be no rule about how an individual goes through the door to a new life, it is a true generalisation that, unless as happens with some older and deeply knit couples one death succeeds another, it is necessary and good to face the opening of a different life.

Much help is needed and the 'after-care' of the bereaved is not something which ends with a short spell of mourning. Some are more resilient than others, some seem psychologically incapable of stepping through the door. Yet both the loved one mourned and God who is Life and Love would want the dying to bring forth fruit rather than to spread despondency and decay.

And indeed there should be a steady encouragement towards new life together with the likelihood that there can be a whole new range of activity and interest. It sometimes sounds callous to say that the death of a partner or a close relative can 'release' someone. Yet it may do so, not because there has been an unpleasant restriction before, but simply because dying does lead to resurrection. It is sad when some seem to think that this is somehow disrespectful to the memory of love, and I hope anyone coming to grips with living after another's death will quickly grasp the living nature of the other's continued being—even though this may take concentration, prayer, and a new kind of faith, deeper and more real than ever lived before. If this is grasped, then however difficult, lonely, or at first barren, the new life may seem, it will grow and blossom.

I do not write this idly, but with great purpose, because I have watched with delight the transformation which can and does take place in individual people, who themselves felt they would never get over a loss, and later become such full and lovely members of society, neighbours and pillars of strength to their friends and families that one can only rejoice. Here indeed death is not an end but a new beginning.

DYING

The fifteen-year-old boy I spoke of earlier was very near death when he said he would not mind dying if I was dying too. That night, I slept in a bed alongside his, or rather lay there, because the cancer home he was in was under-staffed, and they asked me not to leave him. We talked quite a lot, and then much of the time he was not wanting more than that I should be there; he put out his hand to stop me, if I moved away, even to go to the lavatory.

But at one point in the night, he spent quite a lot of time saying: Jesus . . . Jesus . . . long pause . . . Jesus. After a while, he turned his head to me and put out his hand and shook me. 'I'm not swearing', he said, 'I'm praying'.

Later, the following day, he said to me: 'I'm dying now'. I nodded and tried to say something, but was choked. He looked at me and said: 'Why are you crying? There's nothing to cry about.' And after that, I said to him I was sad at his going, but would he do something for me. I asked him would he pray for his father, for his brother and sisters, when he got to heaven. Then I said: Will you also pray for me and for all those I try to help during the course of my life? 'Yes', he said, 'I'll do all that.'

That evening, soon after I had come back to see him, and with his uncle on the other side of the bed, he gently went to his Mother and to God, without fear, and conscious till the last moment.

A dear friend of mine who had married comparatively late in life, had spent much of his life in the Sudan, and had acquired an enlarged heart, and frequent bouts of heart failure. His wife and I and he often prayed together, had Mass in his home, and eventually came to hospital together on a particularly bad heart failure. As he lay in considerable pain in the hospital bed, with myself on one side and his wife on the other, various doctors and nurses were doing all they could to relieve the pain. Then one doctor came to him and said he was going to give him an injection and this would make him better. His reply was straight, simple and moving. He said: 'Don't do that. I want to go to God.' Then he turned his head to his wife, and looked lovingly at her and said: 'I love you very much, but I want to go to God'.

He was injected, and he survived a little, so that the two of them spent a night of real joy together in the hospital, while they talked quietly and happily of the past, their life together and their love. When I arrived about six in the morning to see how they were, he had just quietly breathed his last, and I was able to give her Communion at his bedside and pray there with her. I have never seen such a wonderful mingling of deep sorrow, complete love and from her a real joy that he was now with God to whom he had longed to go. His love for her still warms her over the years, years which have been most fruitfully blossoming in relationship with others of all ages who gain immeasurably from her tranquillity and faith.

Some time ago, the matron of a hospital asked me to smile at, and gradually make friends with, a woman who had terminal cancer. She was youngish, and had a husband and two sons in their teens. She was not RC and indeed not religious, and nor were the family.

Starting with a casual 'hello', which I normally try to give in any hospital ward, I got gradually to spending an extra bit of time by her bed, then to sitting talking, got to meet the family, and became real friends with a very lovely person.

It was only really after weeks or even months that I felt able to be more open about prayer, and this came through her beginning to open, to understand, I think, that I was interested in her and the family, and above all that I had time just to be with her a bit.

Once the ice was broken a little, we were soon in clear water. We did not have to talk much about sickness, dying or death itself. We did cover it at first fearfully and later with openness and acceptance. But once we both knew and knew we knew, there wasn't anything much to linger on, but in a way, we all began to live more fully . . . she, her family, myself, the hospital staff.

And when she came to death, there was peace and a wonderful acceptance from her husband and family. He asked that she might be buried from our church, and there was a wonderful togetherness in the sadness, and also in the joy at her release. The mourning came out as a bruise comes out, and in coming out, the pain was more quickly dissipated, and the new life faced in a new way began more serenely.

I have given these few examples. I could give many more. They are simple, undramatic, but they are true and they are real. I have no doubt at all that they were also dignified and completed the person who went through the gates of death, adding too a new dimension to those who shared at the bedside.

For, if there is knowledge which can be shared, then there is no need to fear visiting or having home the dying person, because knowledge shared can be stored away, and life can continue to be lived. And when this happens it is amazing and wonderful to see the person growing, sometimes through a self-centredness towards a peace and concern for others, breathing calmness and a memory which it is sweet to hold after their death, despite the loss and the pain.

For those of the family or friends who come to a situation of being part of a situation of dying, the being prepared to be there is one of the most important functions. It is not always easy to know what to say or what to do, but I suppose the answer is to be yourself and not to put on masks or false brightness. To be truly loving is to be real. And I would fancy that it is more especially necessary to be about if there are lapses from consciousness. It was, in my opinion, a very penetrating scene in a novel by Graham Greene when one of the characters is dying in hospital; he regains consciousness; there is a nurse down the ward; he hears in the distance the beginning of the wireless news . . . and there is no one beside his bed . . .

I have spoken to a great number of people who have been through hospital, I have been in hospital myself as a patient, and I have visited often down the years. Over and over again, the fear that comes out is a fear of *dying alone*. And, sadly, the fear in this case is enhanced, because it has been the experience of many that they have been in a ward when others have died alone. Now, I do not know what can be done about this, because I am not 'part of' the hospital system, but I do know that if I had any power of persuasion, I would want every matron of every hospital to train the staff to do all in their power to be sure that no one ever died alone. I do know one hospital where the matron made that boast to me that no one ever died alone. Whatever my personal trust in God, or resignation, or even wish to die, I think I would like to die in that hospital, or somewhere where I am pretty confident I will not die alone—if God allows it.

It is so hard for us to know what is felt or heard or even dimly penetrates the consciousness of a seemingly unconscious person. Only recently, I was called over to hospital to a man I had been visiting regularly. The nurse said on the phone he did not have long to live. When I got there, I asked how long and she thought perhaps only ten minutes. She and I went to his bedside. He was unconscious. I took his hand, bent over him and said very distinctly that I was there and was going to say the Lord's Prayer with him. When I began, his mouth moved to the shape of the words 'Our Father', and before I had finished he had slipped away in utter peace and serenity, in a way which deeply moved both the nurse and myself.

I do not think there is much more that I can say, except that there is a struggle for some people. That we must face. But for the majority in my experience, there is a gentleness about dying, and a gentleness much emphasised by closeness and attention of loved ones, hospital staff and people like chaplains or priests.

The 'something' which a priest has to 'give' was summed up to me by a deputy matron of a geriatric home who called me in one day. He began his preamble by saying he was an atheist and intensely disliked Roman Catholics. Then, from there, he went on to say that in the home there came a time with each person when there was nothing more medically which could be done . . . death was inevitable. And, he said, though I don't believe, I know there is something you have which we have not. We can do no more at a certain stage . . . I want to be able to call you in at that point . . . they can do with you then.

But it is also important that we just give ourselves. Some keep away from the dying. They say they cannot bear to see them suffer, or something like that. But . . . your not being there does not relieve the sick person of pain or fear or anything . . . it only benefits you, because you have escaped sharing.

We must learn just to be there, literally to be 'in touch'. Words do not matter: silence is healing when it is steeped in love. Avoiding being beside a person as he or she dies is like avoiding the knowledge of the dying, concealing what is happening. To be there is to enter into the most intimate moment of human living—the moment of dying. I wonder if it sounds strange to you to say that I have found in being beside the bed of many who have died over the years that I am closer to them at that moment than any other, and that their memory remains greener for me than any others in whose dying I have not shared so closely.

I do realise that this is not always possible, and I am only holding the suggestion out, because I fancy there are those who stay away from fear, when in reality, though there may be intense suffering, there is really nothing to fear which love cannot, and does not, overcome.

MOURNING

It is one of the great glories of our being as men and women and children that we can cry. One of the other great glories is that we can laugh. In between, there is a whole range of feeling and experience, woven into all that we are as sensitive and intelligent persons, with the power to know and to love.

When we become attached through knowledge to a person, we quite naturally come also to love that person. It is not an absolutely necessary follow-through, but a pretty likely one.

Now, if knowledge is followed by love, and love involves the whole of a person, there is bound to be a terrific shock to the system when the loved one comes under sentence of death and/or dies.

There is a danger at this point that the English background inheritance of the 'stiff upper lip' or the 'closedness' which rules personal feelings and even personal relationships will damage us individually and collectively.

So often, when death occurs it is almost imposed by surrounding society that the husband/wife, son/daughter, parent/child will be expected *not* to cry, not to express any emotion, to bottle up all feeling and to fit into the pattern which will say: Wasn't she wonderful—so calm and brave; not even a tear.

Yet, tears and the release of pent up emotions are immensely valuable and therapeutic. There is no question of tears being soppy or sentimental or childish. Tears and emotions are real and if they express reality, and are not just cooked-up for the occasion, can be wonderfully useful, fruitful and in the long term 'happy-making'.

After all, if you have been close to someone, and perhaps over a long period, whatever your belief in the next world or non-belief, the actual physical, mental and affectionate separation appears total. For this to be accepted with a dead-pan expression, without tears, with stoic fortitude may be fine from the point of view of some philosophies. From the angle of the followers of Christ it is so much eyewash, and a dangerous eyewash at that!

We should never forget the lovely passage in St John's gospel when Lazarus is sick and dies. We are told 'Jesus wept', and the people round about have that wonderful reaction 'See how he loved him'.

We need the opportunity for weeping, for emotional outburst. We need to be unashamed, and indeed rather proud that we are weeping for one we loved and still love.

Of course there is danger that we can be selfish in our expression, but then we are a bit selfish, aren't we? In a way, some expression of our selfish-self is not all bad. But it is important that it flows out rather than coming round in a circle and getting self-centred and destructive.

In our society, today, we are not best adapted to grief and mourning. I myself live in an area where there are various countries of origin and various cultures. I personally first found the Irish tradition of the wake a very strange affair, after a rather English upbringing. It is true that there can be excesses and that it is necessary, as it were, to get into the cultural pattern before really understanding and being able to appreciate. But as time has gone on, I have come to appreciate the closeness and familiarity with death and the dead person, which is to me the essence of the wake. Sitting round at home, with the coffin open, with food and drink flowing freely, with relatives, friends, acquaintances and local dignitaries coming in and out has a reality and a community dimension which is both comforting and releasing.

For the nearest and dearest, the grief is most profound. It can become an almost intolerable strain over a period of hours, or sometimes even days, if only one or two are there in support. But, if a whole stream of people are passing through, each one wanting in a hug or a kiss or a word or a presence to get across: 'I'm sorry. I really do care. He/She was wonderful!' . . . then this aids the bereaved and allows frequent expression of sorrow, which would be a strained repetition with a small circle.

I am sorry, therefore, to find this expression less common today among the Irish. But in this area where I live, the custom is strong for those originating from the Caribbean, and the amount of support which comes at all stages of life, but especially in bereavement from the West Indian community for their friends and neighbours is beautiful and very valuable. In this area especially, we have much to learn in our colder, more detached, more isolated behaviour.

For there is a very real and sadly damaging reaction which many neighbours have (or even relatives) . . . it is the reaction to stay away. A home where there has been a death, instead of bursting into new and supportive life, becomes a 'forbidden area', a zone of loneliness and almost ostracism. I am sure that neighbourhoods, churches and particularly relatives must work and be encouraged to work towards a more healthy, more open, more loving way of behaving.

Of course, some of this comes because we say we do not know what to say, we are embarrassed. Then we can cook up a self-justifying idea that 'they' would want to be alone, not to be disturbed and so on. But we may not realise the power, the warmth and the strength which comes from even an inarticulate presence. You do not have to have wonderful phrases of condolence. What is probably needed is inarticulate you, squeezing a hand, giving a hug, getting out half a sentence . . . but obviously caring deeply.

It is also true that far from needing to avoid mention of the person who has died, it is normally very useful and therapeutic for the relative or relatives to reminisce, if they can do so, because all this kind of exchange continues the reality of the existence of the person, which we as Christians would believe to be true and real anyhow. And it brings us to the kind of point where we can remember in Scripture that the angels who were at the tomb said to those who came: 'Why look among the dead for someone who is alive'. That was said of Jesus, but we believe it to be true of our own relations and friends and all who have been created by God, not just for this life, but for eternal life, where we know the one true God and Jesus Christ whom he has sent.

HOPE

It may well seem that much of what I have written is tinged with fatalism, and can therefore be rather sad and depressing. I hope this is not so, because the sense should be that when we live life by facing whatever is in store, we live more fully, even if the future prospect is not too hopeful.

One of the peculiarities of Christian living is that whoever professes to be a follower of Jesus Christ is at once the follower of one who spent a great deal of his time going from place to place healing the sick and casting out devils and even raising dead people to life.

This leads some Christians to the claim that Jesus wants every single person to be cured of any disease they have. There has always been a ministry of healing in the church, and this has been developing a great deal recently, especially under the influence of the Spirit, through the pentecostal or charismatic movements in different parts of the world.

I am not intending to go into this aspect, because there are many other books written specifically on healing. But I want to say two things about the question, and then to talk more generally.

Firstly, I have come across very remarkable 'cures' and also 'respites', many of which have been attributed directly to prayer and faith. These are actual happenings. Their purpose is to me mysterious. It is evident that they are only 'temporary', long as that 'temporary' may be in extension . . . temporary because each of us comes to the point of death and dies at some time. However often we are healed, so far there has always been death ahead. Therefore, while personally wanting to encourage any person to faith and hope in God's healing hand being stretched out, I want also to put in the clause: Thy will not mine be done . . . with an understanding that somehow sickness and death, and healing of course, all come into God's will. What this all means . . . well I find I can only come to some sort of reconciliation by allowing God to deepen the darkness and joy of prayer in my life, and in this I know I am not alone.

Secondly, it does seem very possible for a person to take one of two attitudes. It is possible to be ill, turn one's face to the wall, and fade away. And it also seems possible to fight disease. The old phrase 'while there's life there's hope' is lived out in person after person of whom it can be said: He/she should have been dead ages ago. So, for my part, when I find that there is someone who is going to fight through pain and weakness and the apparent inevitability of death, I find there are many ways, great and small to work along with this attitude of faith and hope.

The main thing which seems important in attitude is that, should the disease just go ahead, somehow there must be no turning back into a bitter reflection on un-answered prayer. After all, many quite strange and inexplicable things happen all the time. Often there is nothing so resilient as the human body and spirit, while the main spur should surely be to make the most of life here and now, by entering into everything, the treatment, the life around, the range of interest and activity available, the development of further and deeper relationships. St Teresa of Avila is supposed to have said at one time that she never realised how well she was until she gave up thinking how ill she was.

Not only can this help the sick person, but also it can help those who are around, the family, friends, doctors and nurses. But in my experience, all this is more possible and likely to succeed if the truth is known as fully as possible, and the living, growing and enjoying are real and realistic. There is nothing worse than the attempted cheerfulness which covers worry and distress, and so has to force itself through to give a false front of hope. Hope we should encourage, but with faith as a basis, not untruth.

For those who are not actually suffering the illness, but are close to it, the sensitivity with which they can live for the sick person is the touchstone of a satisfactory behaviour and relationship. There can be no doubt that the inner strengths of character and spiritual understanding and relationship with God are powerful allies in what may be a short sharp need to pull out all the stops, or a long-drawn-out test of patience and love.

It is essential to try to take the other person as he or she is, because each individual, though there may be a pattern, will always go through as an individual. How sensitive we need to be to sense the mood of the other, who one day will be on top of the world and planning next year's summer holiday, and the very next day, or even the same evening, may have given up all hope and be almost collapsed in spirit. In a way, it is often easy to be gay and happy with someone in high spirits; but the degree of cheerfulness and optimism and so on when there is despair and gloom all round—that is the test.

There are some who will not face up to the situation, will not want to know, will apparently pretend that a complete cure is just round the corner . . . as indeed it may be! For each of us to live in hope with them is far better than spending a long time trying to persuade them of the approach of death. A realisation may have been there and been discarded, may genuinely have never been imagined, or may be lurking somewhere. But, a realisation and rejection may be an act of faith and hope which the relative or friend should enter into at the same point of faith as the person suffering.

It is at these times that planning and action may be valuable to both sides. I well recall a very lovely and moving period of many months when I was close to Mary Bonsanquet, a writer, and a wife and mother. She had a clear knowledge of the cancer from which she was suffering. She underwent much medical treatment, and eventually the doctors said they really could not do more for her than ease her suffering. She was both completely realistic about this statement, and also completely realistic in deciding to attempt a nature cure. Reality and hope went hand in hand, and she really entered into the nature treatment with a liveliness and will. Towards the last weeks of her life, we recorded an interview for TV, which was most moving and hope-filled, as she spoke of her loving home relationships and her own growth. She was tired out by the exercise and yet even then full of enthusiasm and interest, an interest further boosted for her by the publication of her life of Bonhoeffer. The family too entered into her zest for living and her calmness at the possibility of dying.

The great usefulness of someone ill who is also full of life seems sometimes to be wasted by us, because we become over-protective. Of course there must be a sensible care, but also a freedom and an encouragement to be active, the move out when possible, to 'receive' others and 'give to' as well as 'get from' the visit. As I write, a young teenage boy who is a mongoloid birth and therefore in some ways mentally handicapped has had a serious relapse. He has a hole in his heart. He is not expected to live more than a year. But a short while ago, he became unconscious, and remained so for a couple of hours. The doctor said there was nothing to be done, and I sat with his mother, after praying and anointing him. Quite suddenly, he regained consciousness, talked lucidly, was weak but fine. I am not here claiming any 'miracle'; what I am interested in is the wonderful relationship which had already a tremendous background, but has now continued to grow—*because of him.* As he regained consciousness, his younger brother came to lie on the bed beside him. Sean said to him, just back in consciousness, unaware of his 'desperate' condition: 'Hello, Bernard, you've been a very good brother to me.' Since then, he has improved beyond all possibility. Time has gone by, he is happy, active, full of life. Though in a way I think he sensed 'death' when he spoke to his brother, now he is alive, and he is happy and he does not even know that he is ill . . . What a wonderful gift from God! For his parents, there is anxiety, wear and tear, questioning, but over all there is a great and wonderful sense of joy, life, purpose and acceptance which makes the waiting period towards a death which the doctors say is inevitable, not only possible, but positively exciting, joyful and something for which they are continually expressing their thanks to God. Though, at this stage, we can none of us see far ahead or what will happen after Sean's death, there is a sound hope that all that is happening now will be held in memory as a rich and beautiful time, where it might have been a bitter, unacceptable evil.

POSTSCRIPT

The thoughts and ideas in these pages are my own, in one form or another. It would be untrue to say they were all original, because I have read a certain amount and listened a certain amount. But I am in no sense a professional, so that I would be very happy to find that people who read what is here were prepared to pick holes and to make suggestions. It is, though, very important to be positive and not simply destructive.

If I had in any way attempted to 'cover' the whole area of sickness, bereavement, mourning, the after life and so on, then I should have required time, space and a breadth of knowledge and even scholarship which are not available. I write as a person living among, concerned with, and loving a number of people of differing ages, sexes, colours, classes, creeds and convictions, who have in common with me the mortality of the human being. Some of them have found not only comfort but growth in the line of reasoning, believing and living which is shown in the previous pages. I know that there are others whom I have not helped.

The life of a jack-of-all-trades is fascinating. It is also demanding and leaves less time than would be pleasant for the kind of respite, thinking, reading and just being with God, which I would consider basic to understanding and helping other people. For me, perhaps for so many people today, this is a serious problem, and our breakdown and dissatisfaction is in no small part due to our own personal unease and frustration and lack of stillness.

Because of pressure, we allow others to become cases or beds or numbers or patients.

This is in itself a sickness in our society and in ourselves. If the old saying is 'physician heal thyself', today we need to re-emphasise this, to extend it to 'man know thyself', and to give only partial assent to the findings of a psychology which limits the existence and range of the soul.

A person is a person is a person. We must be personal. In this there is great help in believing in a personal God, who loves you with an everlasting love, and who has made his creation from his own love, so that his creation man is in essence a loving being, though bedevilled by aggression, jealousy and distrust.

Now, there are some individual people and groups who are 'specialising' in care for the sick and dying, in a way which is (if I may put it that way) medical/psychological/hospital *plus*. Such a person I would single out in Dr Cecily Saunders of St Christopher's, such a group as the sisters and team at St Joseph's, Hackney. There are other places and people. These I know best by experience and reputation.

There are many too who have written about all aspects much more fully than I have. Again, I cannot give a comprehensive list, but I would like to suggest that these names which follow are among the valuable materials available to help professional and un-professional alike to live with, work with, love and care for our friends and neighbours, or kith and kin who are undergoing the common human lot of suffering.

There has been a mushroom-growth of interest and practical development in care for the dying. The Hospice movement has taken off. Many people are publishing their thought and experience in this whole area. Here I can give only a few pointers. Always ask, because there is a lot of good material available today.

Care of the Dying, (second edition) Cicely Saunders (Macmillan Journals Ltd. 1976).

Death and the Family, Lily Pincus (Faber & Faber Ltd. 1976).

Death, Grief and Mourning, G. Gorer (Cresset Press).

The Moment of Truth, Ladislaus Boros (Burns Oates).

Dying, (second edition) John Hinton (Pelican 1972).

The Shade of his Hand, Hollings and Gullick (Mayhew-McCrimmon).

Living With Grief, Dr Tony Lake (Sheldon Press, SPCK, 1984).

The Pain That Heals, Dr Martin Israel (Mowbray, 1981).

On Children and Death, Elisabeth Kubler-Ross (Macmillan, 1983). NB: There are numerous titles by this author which are worth reading.

Before Death Comes, Dr Maurice Rawlings (Sheldon, 1980).

Counselling the Dying, Edgar N. Jackson (Ed) (Nelson, 1981).

Letting Go — Caring for the Dying and Bereaved, Ian Ainsworth and Peter Speck (SPCK, 1982).

PRAYERS

How do I love thee? Let me count the ways.
I love thee to the depth and breadth and height
my soul can reach, when feeling out of sight.
For the ends of Being and ideal Grace
I love thee to the level of every day's
most quiet need, by sun and candlelight.
I love freely, as men strive for right;
I love thee purely as they turn from Praise.
I love thee with the passion put to use
in my old griefs, and with my childhood's faith.
I love thee with a love I seemed to lose
with my lost saints—I love thee with the breath,
smiles, tears, of all my life, and if God choose,
I shall but love thee better after death.

Elizabeth Barrett Browning

Lord, my loved ones are near me.
I know that they live in the shadow.
My eyes can't see them because they have left for a moment their bodies as one leaves behind outmoded clothing.
Their souls, deprived of their disguise, no longer communicate with me.

But in you, Lord, I hear them calling me,
I see them beckoning to me,
I hear them giving me advice;
For they are now more vividly present.
Before, our bodies touched but not our souls.
Now I meet them when I meet you,
I receive them when I receive you,
I love them when I love you.
O, my loved ones, eternally alive, who live
in me,
help me to learn thoroughly in this short life
how to live eternally.
Lord, I love you, and I want to love you more.
It's you who make love eternal, and I want
to love eternally.

Michel Quoist

Teach me, only teach, Love,
as I ought;
I will speak thy speech, Love,
think thy thought—
Meet if thou require it,
both demands,
laying flesh and spirit
in thy hands.
That shall be tomorrow,
not tonight;
I must bury sorrow
out of sight:
Must a little weep, love,
(foolish me!)
and so fall asleep, love,
loved by thee.

Part of a Robert Browning poem

Like the deer that thirsts for water,
O God I long for you.
Weeping, I have heard them taunt me:
'What help is in your God?'

Gladly I would lead your people,
rejoicing to your house.
Trust in God, my soul and praise him.
and he will dry your tears.

Grief and pain, like roaring torrents,
had swept my soul away.
But his mercy is my rescue,
I praise him all my days.

Weeping, I have heard them taunt me:
'What help is in your God?'
Rock of strength, do not forget me,
in you alone I trust.

To the Father praise and honour,
all glory to the Son,
honour to the Holy Spirit;
let God be glorified.

Psalm 41 paraphrased by Luke Connaughton and Kevin Mayhew

In the hour of my distress,
when temptations me oppress,
and when I my sins confess,
sweet Spirit comfort me!

When I lie within my bed,
sick in heart and sick in head,
and with doubts discomforted,
sweet Spirit comfort me!

When the house doth sigh and weep,
and the world is drawn in sleep,
yet mine eyes the watch do keep;
sweet Spirit comfort me!

When (God knows) I'm tossed about,
either with despair or doubt;
yet before the glass be out,
sweet Spirit comfort me!

When the judgment is reveal'd,
and that open'd that was seal'd,
when to thee I have appeal'd
sweet Spirit comfort me!

Robert Herrick (1591-1674)

Though I am dead grieve not for me with
tears,
think not of death with sorrowing and tears;
I am so near that every tear you shed touches and
tortures me though you think me dead.
But when you laugh and sing in glad delight,
my soul is lifted upward to the light.
Laugh and be glad for all that life is giving and I,
though dead, will share your joy in living.

Anonymous

For rest and peace

O Lord, who art the shadow of a great rock in a weary land, who beholdest thy weak creatures, weary of labour, weary of pleasures, weary of heart from hope deferred, and weary of self. In thine abundant compassion and unutterable tenderness bring us we pray thee, unto thy rest, through Jesus Christ, thy Son, our Saviour.

Christina Rossetti (1830-1895)

Death, be not proud, though some have called
thee
mighty and dreadful, for thou art not so;
For those, whom thou think'st thou dost
overthrow,
die not, poor Death . . .
one short sleep past, we wake eternally.
And Death shall be no more: Death thou shalt
die.

John Donne (1573-1631)

O thou in whose house are many mansions, speak through me to those whose loved one has gone from their sight, but not from thine. There is nothing in me to heal the wounded heart or fill the aching void. But let thy words of comfort and truth be given to me to speak that these sorrowing ones may find their peace in thee; through Jesus Christ our Lord.

Prayers for the Minister's Day

The fall doth pass the rise in worth:
for birth hath in itself the germ of death,
but death has in itself the germ of birth.
It is the falling acorn buds the tree,
the falling rain that bears the greenery;
the fern plants moulder when the ferns arise,
for there is nothing lives but something dies.
And there is nothing dies but something lives,
till skies be fugitives.

Francis Thompson

Remember me when I am gone away,
gone far away into the silent land;
When you can no more hold me by the hand,
nor I half turn to go yet turning stay.
Remember me when no more day by day
you tell me of our future that you planned;
Only remember me; you understand
it will be late to counsel then or pray.
Yet if you should forget me for a while
and afterwards remember, do not grieve;
For if the darkness and corruption leave
a vestige of the thoughts that once I had,
better by far you should forget and smile
than that you should remember and be sad.

Christina Rossetti (1830-1895)

It is right to weep and mourn
but not for yourself
for they have gone to a better place.
The tears release the tension;
take courage—remember happy days
you shared—and though you are sad
carry on as they would have you,
living, loving, laughing, caring,
God is with you though you may not know it.
He will help you through your lonely days;
just open your heart and let Him in.

Unknown

O Lord,
who healest the broken-hearted
and bindest up their wounds,
grant thy consolation unto mourners.

O strengthen and support them
in their day of grief and sorrow;
and remember them (and their children)
for a long and good life.
Put into their hearts the fear and love of thee;
that they may serve thee with a perfect heart
and let their latter end be peace.

From the Jewish 'Authorised Daily Prayer Book'

Earthy condition is essentially that of
wayfarers,
of completeness, moving towards fulfilment
and therefore a struggle.

Yves Congar

The depth of darkness into which you can
descend
and still live,
is an exact measure, I believe,
of the height to which you can aspire
to reach.

Alan McGlashan

Love is not changed by death
—and nothing is lost,
and all in the end is harvest.

Edith Sitwell

He whom we love and lose
is no longer where he was before.
He is now wherever we are.

John Chrysoston

Death is not extinguishing the Light
but putting out the Lamp because the dawn
has come.

R. Tagore

Some other books by Michael Hollings

GO IN PEACE
ISBN 0 85597 375 7
Father Hollings explores the place of confession in the Church as part of an open, loving relationship with God.

LIVING PRIESTHOOD
ISBN 0 85597 110 X
Father Hollings formulates his ideas on what it means to him to be a priest in the modern parish.

PATH TO CONTEMPLATION
ISBN 0 85597 357 9
'An extraordinary booklet which deals with the essentials of a subject which has filled innumerable volumes down the centuries.' — *The Universe*.

THE ONE WHO LISTENS
(with Etta Gullick)
ISBN 0 85597 376 5
A completely revised and updated edition of this best-selling collection of prayers covering all aspects of human experience.

Some other books by Michael Hollings

GO IN PEACE
ISBN 0 85597 175 [illegible]
Father Hollings explores the place of confession in the Church as part of an ever-growing relationship with God.

LIVING PRIESTHOOD
ISBN 0 85597 110 X
Father Hollings formulates his ideas on what it means to him to be a priest in the modern parish.

PATH TO CONTEMPLATION
ISBN 0 85597 [illegible]
"An extraordinary booklet which deals with the essentials of a subject which has filled innumerable volumes down the centuries" — *The Universe*

THE ONE WHO LISTENS
(with Etta Gullick)
ISBN 0 85597 [illegible] 5
A completely revised and updated edition of the best-selling collection of prayers covering all aspects of human experience.